4-WAY COORDINAT

By MARVIN DAHLGREN
Percussionist—Minneapolis Symphony • Instructor—University of Minnesota

And ELLIOT FINE
Percussionist—Minneapolis Symphony

A Method Book for
the Development of
Complete Independence
on the DRUM SET

TABLE OF CONTENTS

Introduction

This book was written for the drummer interested in developing coordination between both hands and both feet. The development of this technique will lead to complete independence.

A drummer uses both hands and both feet in playing, but until recently the feet have played a subordinate part. The authors feel there is abundant evidence in the playing of many modern drummers to indicate that the future drummer will have to be as proficient with his feet as he is with his hands.

This book assigns exactly as much work to each of the hands and feet. In other words, it will help to develop your feet until they are the equal of your hands.

In order to keep the exercises in this book as easy to read as possible, we have used the following notation:

Notes written above the top line will be played by the right hand (measure A in the example below).

Notes written below the top line will be played by the left hand (measure B in the example below).

Notes written above the bottom line will be played by the right foot (measure C in the example below).

Notes written below the bottom line will be played by the left foot (measure D in the example below).

EXAMPLE OF NOTATION

R. H. –Right hand
L. H. –Left hand
R. F. –Right foot
L. F. –Left foot

A dotted line separates the line used for the hands from the line used for the feet. This makes it easier to practice the hands or feet separately.

HAB19

MELODIC COORDINATION

The first section of this book deals with melodic coordination. The authors use the term melodic coordination to indicate that only one hand or foot is being played at a time.

These exercises are written in 4/4 time and should be practiced slowly at first and gradually worked up to the recommended metronomic marking.

1. Practice each measure separately as in measure A from the example below:

R.H.-Right hand
L.H.-Left hand
R.F.-Right foot
L.F.-Left foot

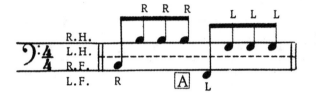

This measure is played Right Foot, Right Hand, R.H., R.H., Left Foot, Left Hand, L.H., L.H.

2. Practice two measures before repeating. In this exercise you will notice the feet remain the same, but the hands in the second measure are the opposite of the hands in the first measure. Start slowly and gradually work up to the recommended metronomic marking.

This exercise could be measure A and B or measure C and D of the example below:

This is how measures A B would be played:

R.H. -Right hand
L.H. -Left hand
R.F. -Right foot
L.F. -Left foot

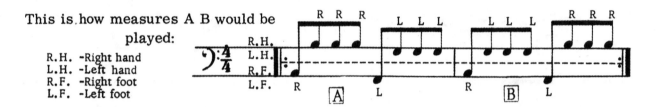

EXAMPLE OF MELODIC COORDINATION:

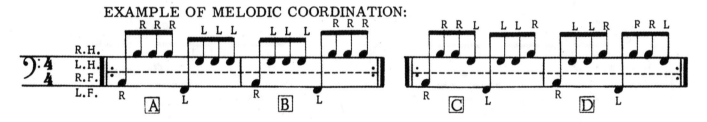

3. Another way to practice melodic coordination is to play two measures of rhythm first and then play two measures of melodic coordination.

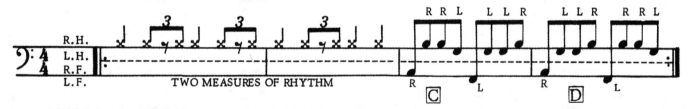

Notice in this exercise we have used measures C and D from the previous example of melodic coordination. In the second measure of rhythm play only a quarter note on the fourth beat to allow more time for changing the right hand to the snare drum or tom tom.

Remember, practice slowly at first. The metronomic marking is not the maximum speed, but represents the tempo any proficient drummer should be able to attain. With diligent practice these exercises can be performed much faster than marked.

Melodic Coordination - Exercises in Eighth Notes

1. Practice each measure separately.
2. Practice in two-measure phrases.
3. Play two measures of rhythm between each two-measure phrase.

HAB19

Eighth Note Solos in Melodic Coordination

1. Play solos as written.
2. Add two measures of rhythm between each solo.

Four-Measure Solos

1. Play solos as written. 2. Add four measures of rhythm between each solo.

8

Eighth Notes - Two-Measure Solos

1. Play solos as written.
2. Play two measures of rhythm between each solo.
3. Combine two solos to form four-measure solos.

Melodic Coordination- Exercises in Triplets

The following page of exercises in melodic coordination consists of all the possible ways of playing triplets. Four triplets are grouped in a box in order to give you six different ways of combining two triplets. In the example, we have lettered the triplets A, B, C and D in order to clarify the six ways to practice these exercises.

EXAMPLE of Melodic Coordination in Triplet Form:

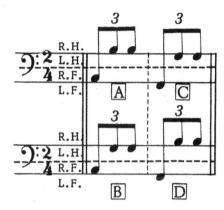

1. Play Triplet A followed by Triplet C: These measures are exact opposites.

2. Play Triplet A followed by Triplet B: Foot remains the same; hands are opposite.

3. Play Triplet A followed by Triplet D: Feet opposite; hands the same.

4. Play Triplet B followed by Triplet C: Feet opposite; hands the same.

5. Play Triplet B followed by Triplet D: Measures are exact opposites.

6. Play Triplet C followed by Triplet D: Foot remains the same; hands are opposite.

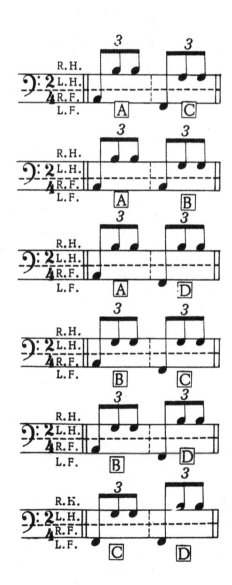

1. Practice each triplet separately.
2. Combine two triplets.
3. Combine four triplets.
4. Play one measure of rhythm between each group of four triplets.

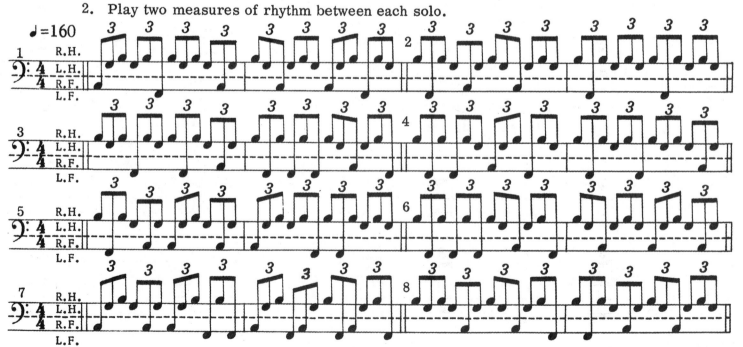

Triplets Solos in Melodic Coordination

1. Practice solos as written.
2. Play two measures of rhythm between each solo.

1. Practice in two-measure phrases.
2. Practice in four-measure phrases.
3. Play rhythm between each phrase.

LONG ROLL TRIPLETS:

SINGLE STROKE TRIPLETS:

PARATRIPLETS (FOOT ON 1st NOTE):

PARATRIPLETS (FOOT ON 2nd NOTE):

PARATRIPLETS (FOOT ON DOUBLES):

HAB19

12

1. Practice in two-measure phrase.
2. Practice in four-measure phrase.
3. Play rhythm between each phrase.

LONG ROLL SEPARATED BY FOOT NOTE (May be thought of as 5-stroke roll)

LONG ROLL SEPARATED BY FOOT NOTE (May be thought of as 7-stroke roll)

SIX STROKE ROLLS:

SINGLE PARADIDDLE SEPARATED BY FOOT NOTE:

DOUBLE FOOT BETWEEN 3-NOTE PATTERN:

PARADIDDLEDIDDLE

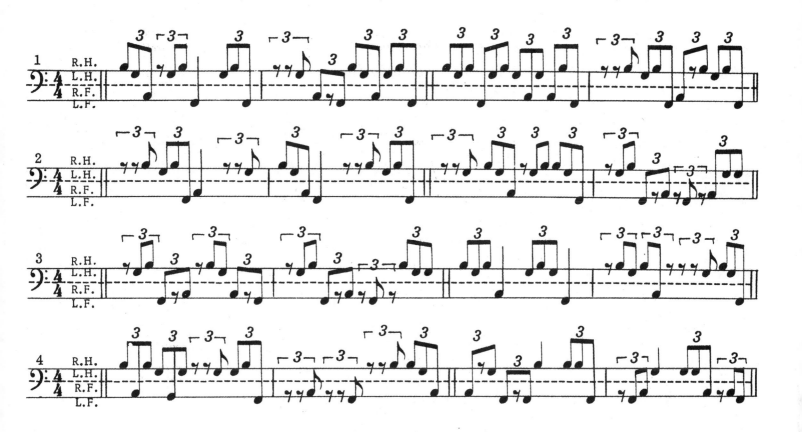

Combining Eighth Notes and Triplets in Solo

1. Practice solos as written.
2. Play four measures of rhythm between each solo.

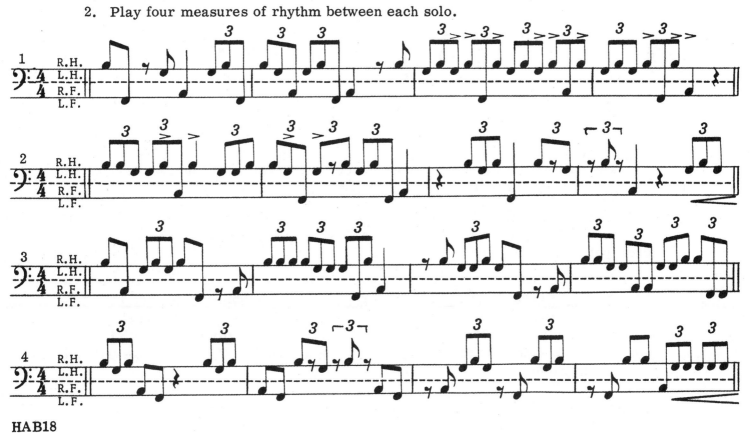

Two Eight-Measure Solos:
1. Practice as written.
2. Play 8 measures of rhythm between each solo.

HARMONIC COORDINATION

The next section is written in harmonic coordination. Harmonic coordination means playing more than one hand or foot at a time.

At first we will be concerned only with 2-PART harmonic coordination. This means we will play one pattern with the hands while the feet play the same or a different pattern.

The exercises are grouped as they were in the melodic coordination section. At the beginning of each set of exercises we have indicated which notes of each four-note group have identical coordination (Right hand with right foot - or - left hand with left foot); and which notes in the group have opposite coordination (Right hand with left foot - or - left hand with right foot). This knowledge will help your coordination until you begin to get the feel of these exercises.

Two-part Harmonic Coordination - Exercises in Eighth Notes

Groups of Four Notes:

1. Practice each group separately.
2. Play two groups to form a 4/4 measure.
3. Play two 4/4 measures to form a two-measure phrase.
4. Play rhythm between each phrase.

A and C (hands and feet are identical) B and D (hands and feet are opposite)

A and C (1st note is identical) B and D (1st note is opposite)

HAB19

Group of Four Notes:
1. Practice each group separately. 2. Practice two groups to form a 4/4 measure.
3. Practice two 4/4 measures to form a two-measure phrase.
A and C (2nd note is identical) B and D (2nd note is opposite)

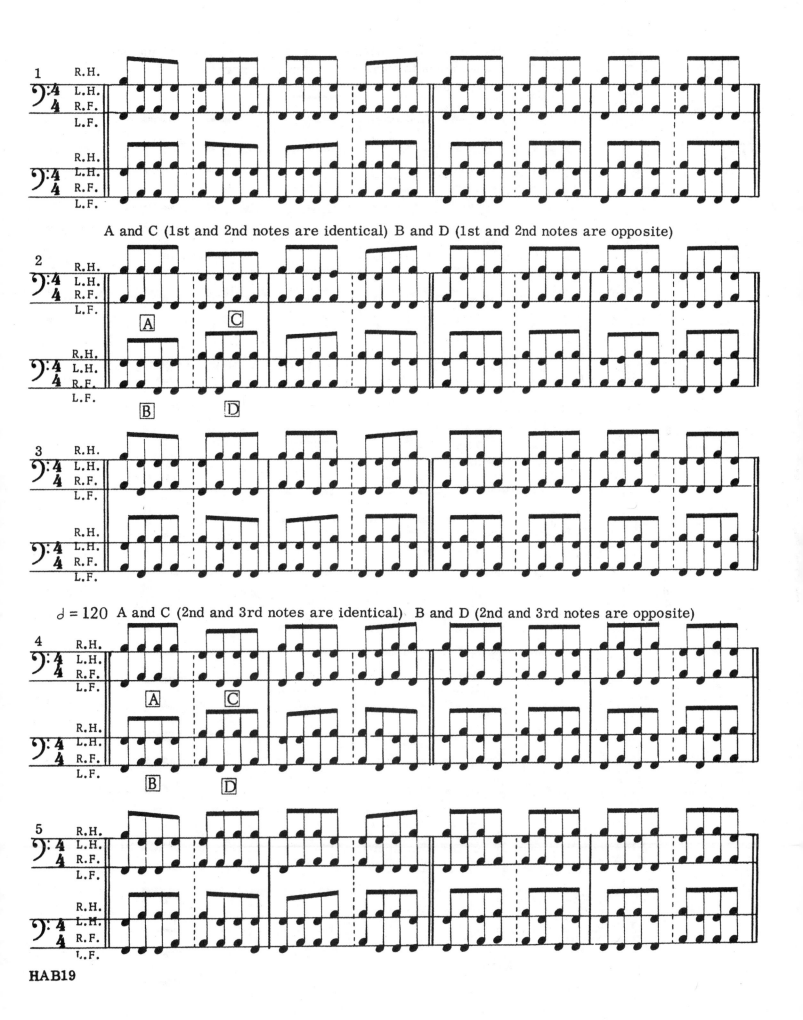

A and C (1st and 2nd notes are identical) B and D (1st and 2nd notes are opposite)

♩ = 120 A and C (2nd and 3rd notes are identical) B and D (2nd and 3rd notes are opposite)

HAB19

A and C (1st and 3rd notes are identical) B and D (1st and 3rd notes are opposite)

Eighth Note Solos in two-part Harmonic Coordination

1. Practice hands alone.
2. Practice feet alone.
3. Play solos as written but without accents.
4. Play two measures of rhythm between each solo.
5. Add accents to solos.

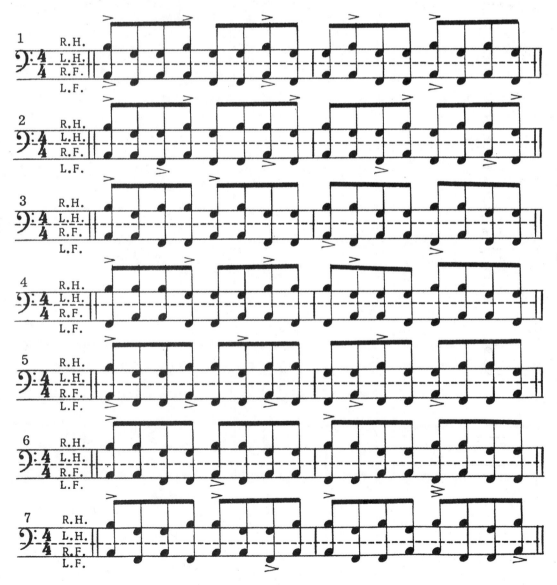

Four-Measure Solos - Eighth Notes

1. Practice hands alone.
2. Practice feet alone.
3. Play solos as written.
4. Play four measures of rhythm between each solo.

HAB19

Two-part Harmonic Coordination - Exercises in Triplets

Triplets:

1. Practice each triplet separately.
2. Combine two triplets.
3. Combine four triplets.
4. Play one measure of rhythm between each group of four triplets.

A and C Identical; B and D Opposite:

A and C (1st Note Identical); B and D (1st Note Opposite):

A and C (2nd Note Identical); B and D (2nd Note Opposite):

A and C (3rd Note Identical); B and D (3rd Note Opposite):

Two- and Four-Measure Solos

LONG ROLL TRIPLETS:

PARATRIPLETS:

HAB19

Notice the next six exercises are in 3/4 time:

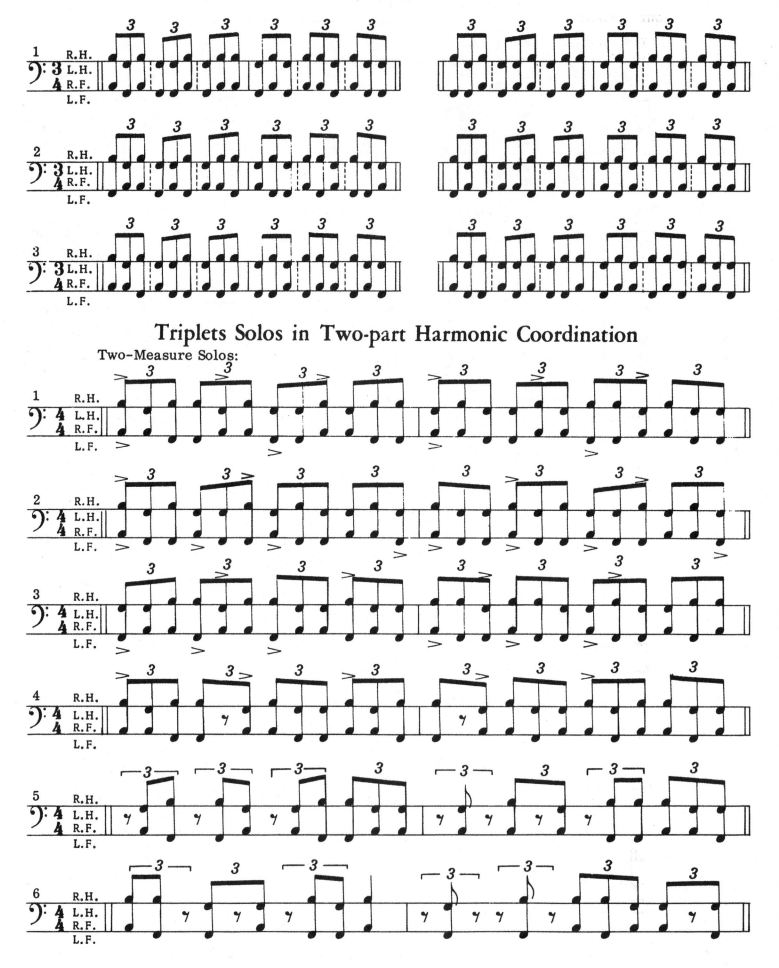

Triplets Solos in Two-part Harmonic Coordination

Two-Measure Solos:

Combining Eighth Notes and Triplets in Solos

Four-Measure Solos

1. Practice solos as written.
2. Play four measures of rhythm between each solo.

Notice the next four exercises are in 3/4 time:

HAB19

FOUR-WAY COORDINATION

In order to gain complete independence, it is necessary to develop the ear to hear more than one rhythm at the same time. The rest of this book deals with playing four rhythms at the same time: one for each hand; one for each foot.

As far as the technique of playing four independent rhythms is concerned, the drummer must feel relaxed and natural whether he is playing with one or two hands or feet or with both hands or feet. To help you feel right regardless of how many limbs are playing, practice the following exercises. In each exercise we start with one hand or foot and end with both hands and both feet being played.

The next few pages combine all the coordination we have developed so far.

Eighth Note Patterns.

1. Practice A and B with the hands. 2. Practice A and B with the feet.

Combine A and B to form 4-way coordination:

1. Practice C through L with the hands. 2. Practice C through L with the feet.

Three Rights; Three Lefts:

As an example: Combine D and K to form 4-way coordination:

Practice Combinations of Your Own Choice.

Eighth Note Triplet Patterns.

1. Practice patterns A through K with the hands. 2. Practice patterns A through K with feet.

Two Rights; Two Lefts:

HAB19

26

Three Rights; Three Lefts:

♩=120

Three Rights; Three Lefts:

This is a combination of I with the hands and E with the feet:

♩=120

G with the hands, B with the feet: J with the hands, A with the feet:

Practice other combinations.

1. Practice A through N with the hands. 2. Practice A through N with the feet.

Three Rights; Two Lefts:

♩=120

Three Lefts; Two Rights:

Three Rights; Two Lefts:

Three Lefts; Two Rights:

Combinations:

Many other combinations may be formed.

Four-way Coordination on the Drum Set

(using the right hand on the ride cymbal)

The following exercises should be played on a set of drums.

When a note is written with an ♩ it means that note should be played on a cymbal. An ♩ on a right hand note should be played on a cymbal mounted a little to the right of the player; an ♩ on a left hand note should be played on a cymbal mounted a little to the left of the player. An ♩ on a left foot note means that note should be played on a hi-sock. The hi-sock should be closed tightly on playing to produce a chick sound <u>except</u> when the note is written with a circle under it ♩. Then it should be released immediately upon playing to produce a ching or ringing sound.

Although the hi-sock is the usual instrument played with the left foot, many drummers have used the left foot to play a second bass drum, a tambourine, sleigh bells or other traps with excellent results. For this reason we use ♩ notes for the left foot only when we wish to utilize the ringing sound of the hi-sock in an exercise. On all other exercises we have used regular notes, even though we realize most drummers will continue to play the hi-sock with the left foot.

The exercises that follow are excellent studies for learning to play patterns with the left foot.

Studies to develop the left foot

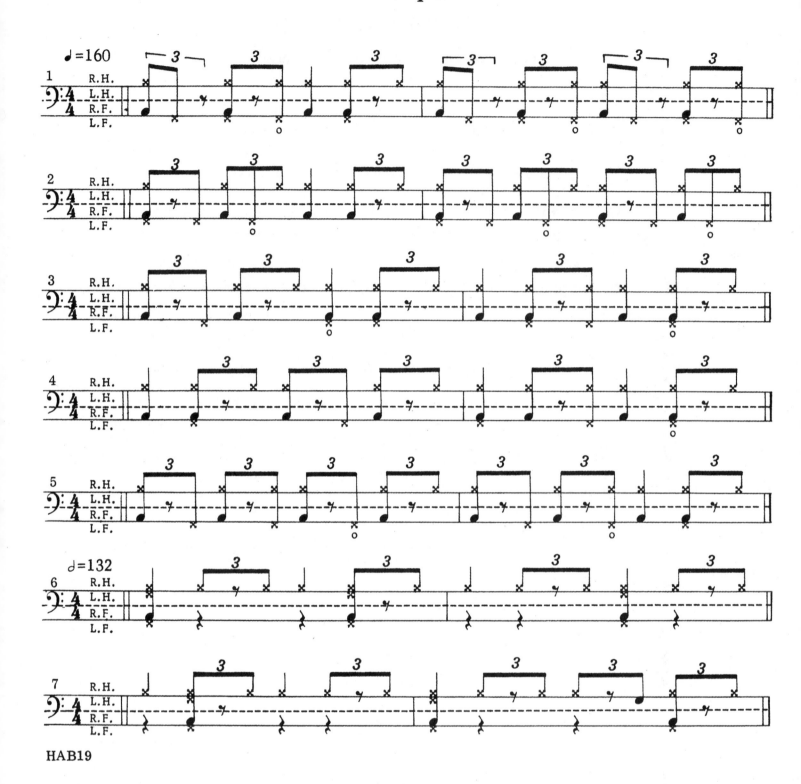

HAB19

The next set of exercises requires left hand independence as well as left foot independence.

The first measure in each exercise is written with the left foot playing in a normal manner. In the second measure the hands and right foot play exactly what they played in the first measure, but the left foot plays a different rhythm than it played in the first measure.

Adding the left hand

The exercises are grouped in 4/4 time; 3/4 time; and 5/4 time.

1. Practice the 1st measure until it is mastered.
2. Practice the second measure until it is mastered.
3. Practice both measures in sequence.
4. Play two measures of rhythm between each exercise.

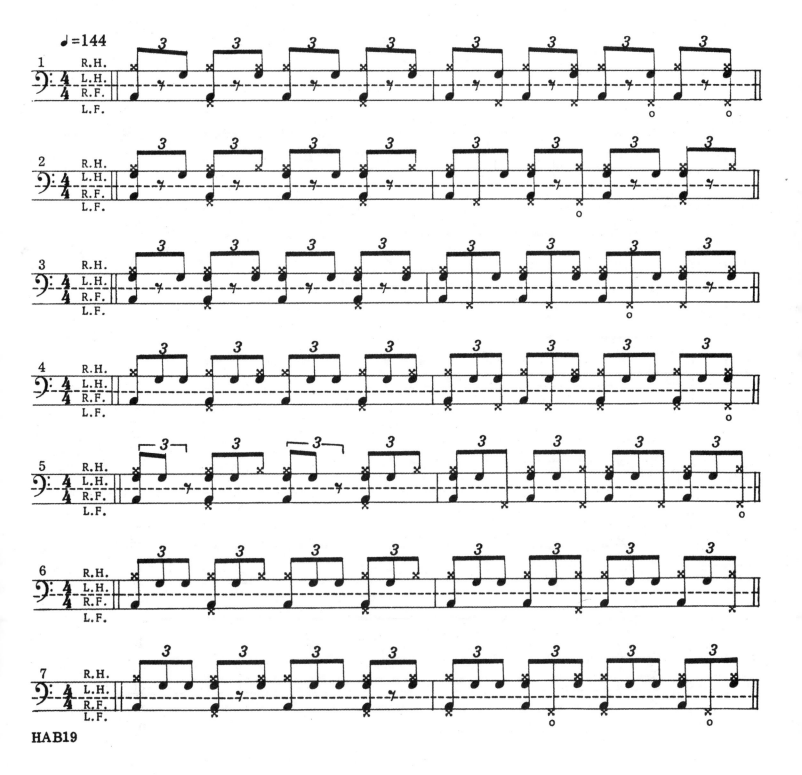

HAB19

COMPLETE INDEPENDENCE

in 2/4, 3/4, 4/4, 5/4 and 6/4 time

Complete independence is the ambition of every serious drummer. With complete independence he will be able to play any pattern he desires with either hand or foot without disturbing the rhythm of his other hand or foot.

On the following pages we have designed a series of exercises to enable you to develop the independence necessary to play countless rhythmic combinations with both hands and feet.

Because of the great variety of time signatures with which a modern drummer is confronted, we have planned our exercises so they may be played in 2/4, 3/4, 4/4, 5/4 or 6/4 time.

Each set of exercises starts with a basic rhythm. This basic rhythm is a combination of the right hand cymbal beat and the two feet and must be mastered first.

On the six lines below each basic rhythm, the left hand has been added in a variety of patterns from simple ones to very complex ones.

The exercises are always written as two measures of 2/4 time followed by two measures of 3/4 time.

In the example below we have lettered the two measures of 2/4 time as measure A and measure B. The two measures of 3/4 time are lettered measure C and measure D.

If you wish to practice 2/4 time, play either the first measure (measure A) or the second measure (measure B).

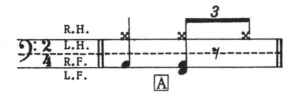

If you wish to practice 4/4 time either repeat the 2/4 measure or play both 2/4 measures (measure A and B together).

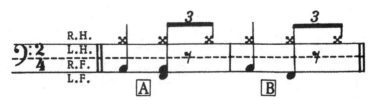

If you wish to practice 3/4 time, play either the third measure (measure C) or the fourth measure (measure D).

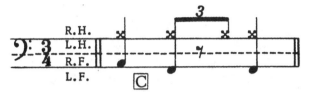

If you wish to practice 6/4 time (or 3/4 time in a two-measure phrase) play measures C and D.

If you wish to practice 5/4 time play measure B and C or measure C followed by measure D up to the dotted line.

Measures B, C should be felt as (2/4, 3/4):

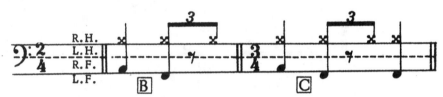

Measure C followed by measure D up to the dotted line should be felt as (3/4, 2/4):

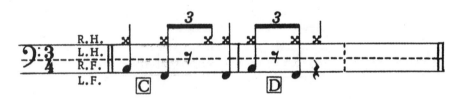

Other combinations may be formed by reading vertically or diagonally as in the exercises on harmonic coordination.

HAB19

34

1. Practice the basic rhythm until it feels natural.
2. Practice the hands alone on the rest of the exercises.
3. Combine hands and feet (in other words, play as written).

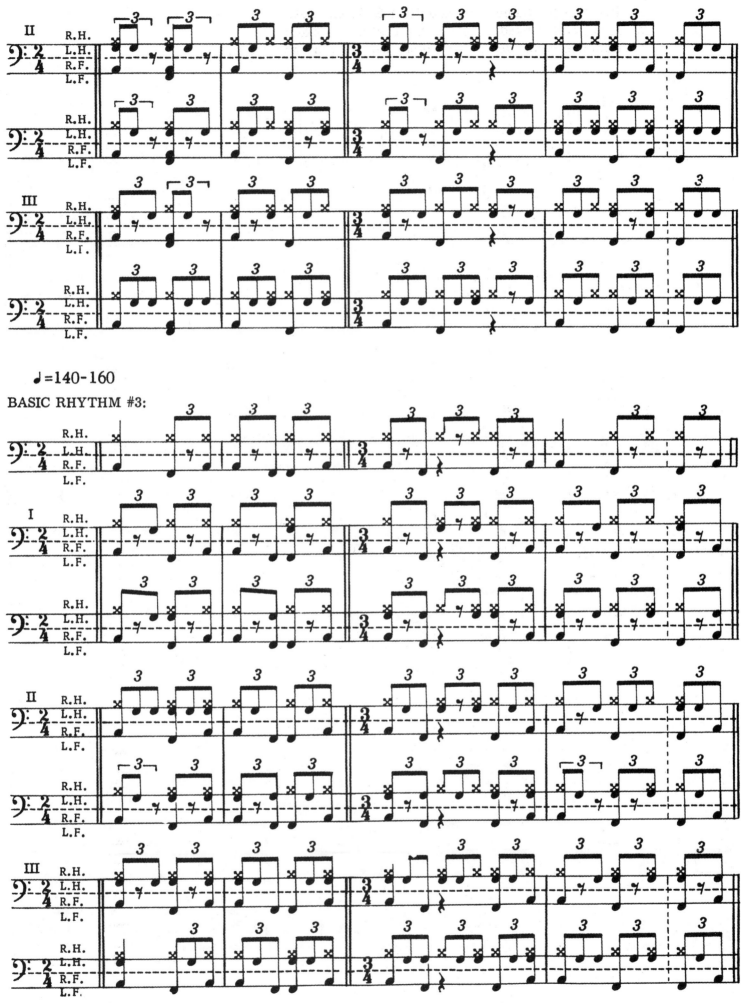

♩=140-160

BASIC RHYTHM #3:

HAB19

BASIC RHYTHM #4:

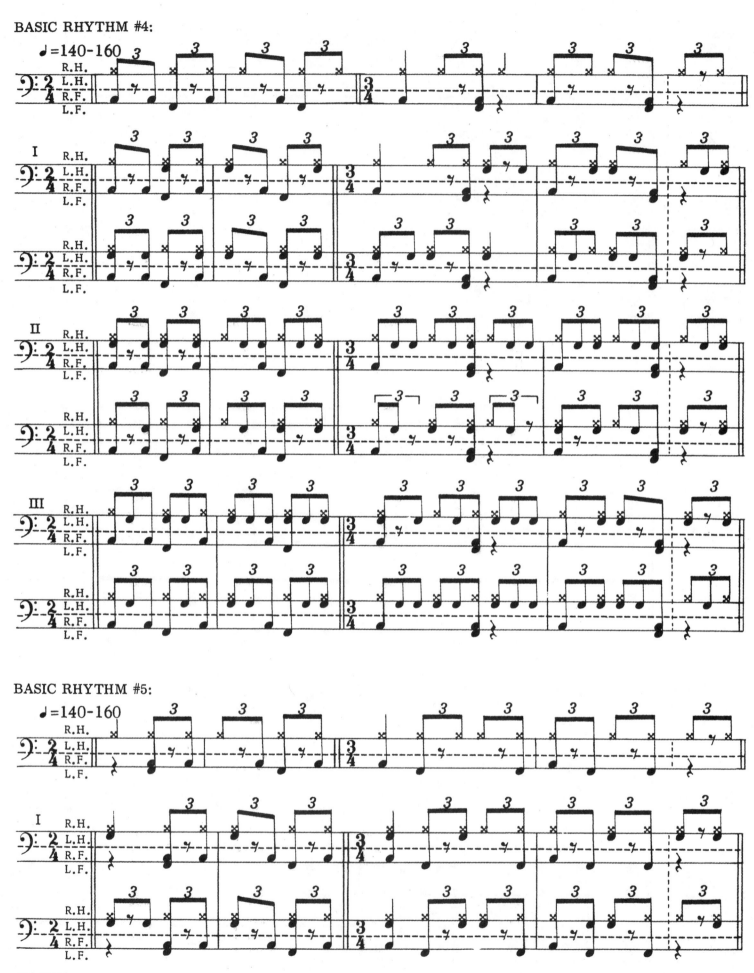

BASIC RHYTHM #5:

HAB19

BASIC RHYTHM #6:

BASIC RHYTHM #7:

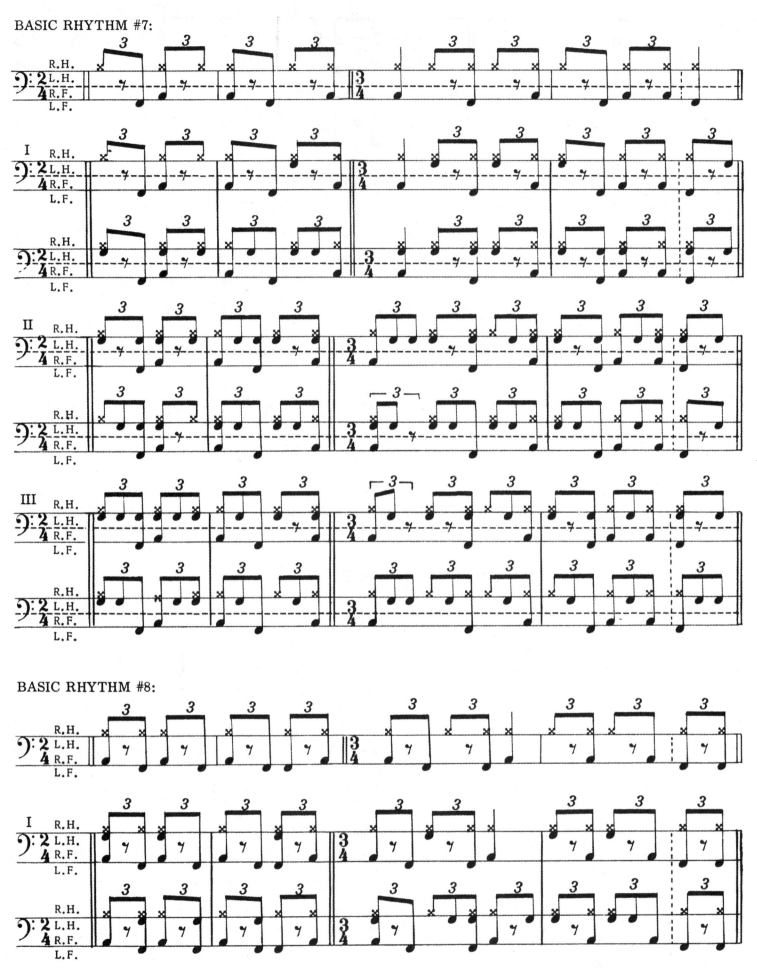

BASIC RHYTHM #8:

HAB19

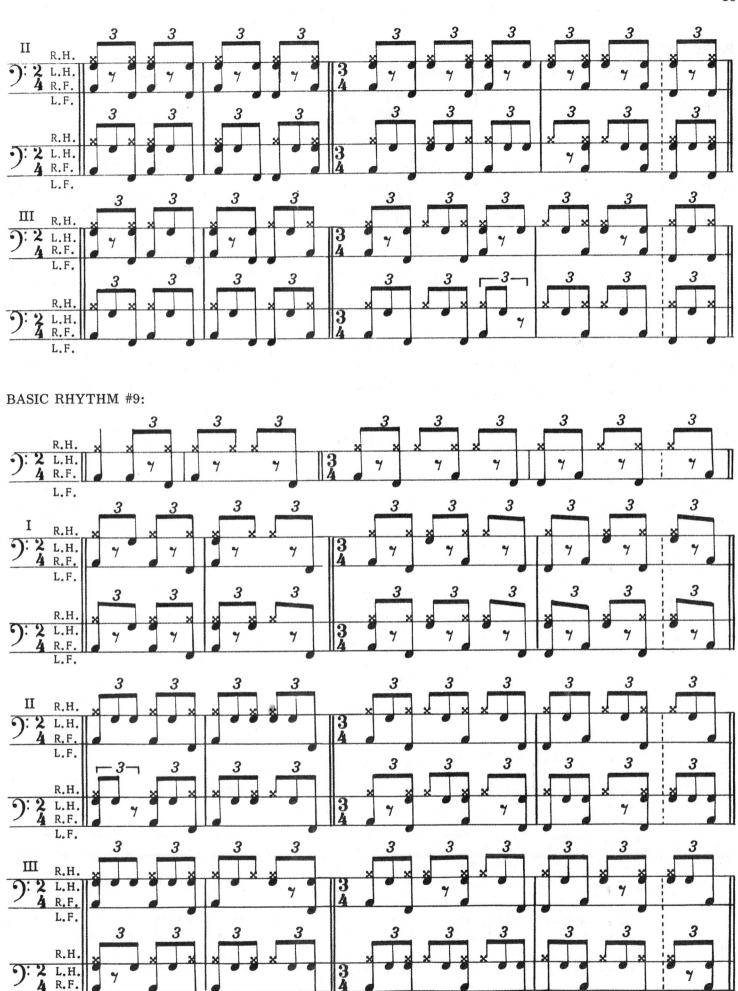

BASIC RHYTHM #9:

BASIC RHYTHM #10:

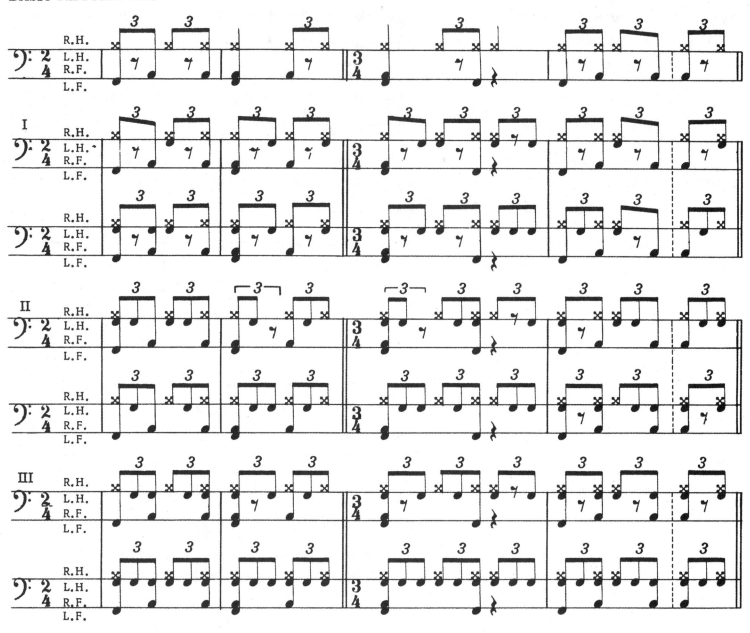

BASIC RHYTHM #11:

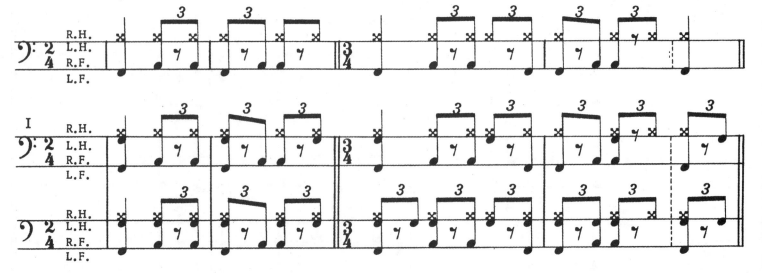

HAB19

BASIC RHYTHM #12:

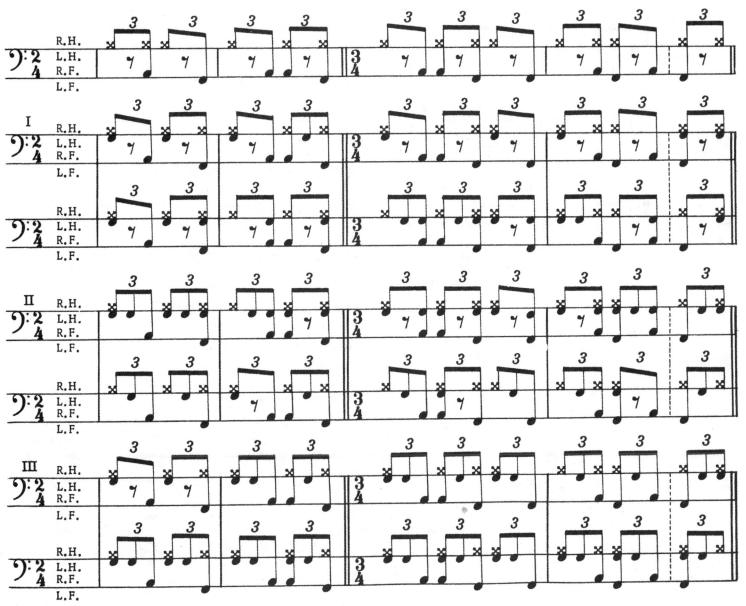

HAB19

BASIC RHYTHM #13:

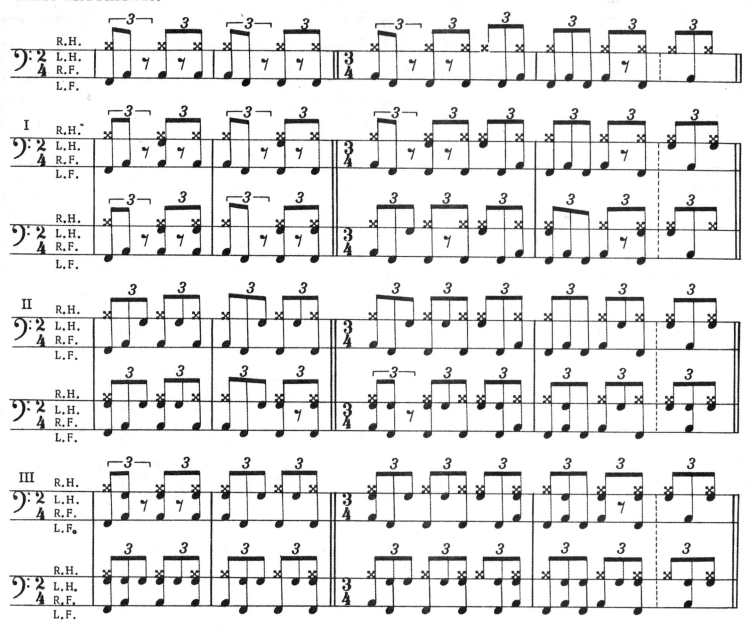

BASIC RHYTHM #14:

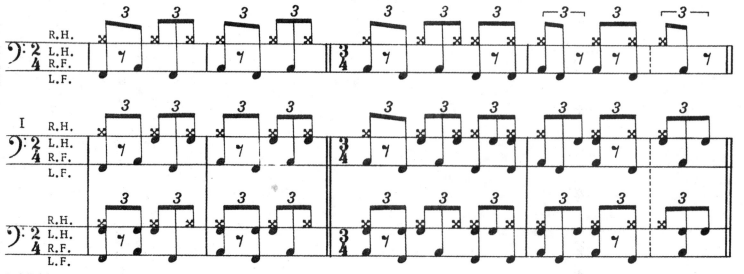

HAB19

BASIC RHYTHM #15:

HAB19

BASIC RHYTHM #16:

BASIC RHYTHM #17:

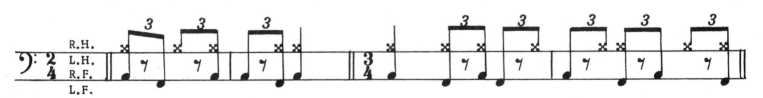

HAB19

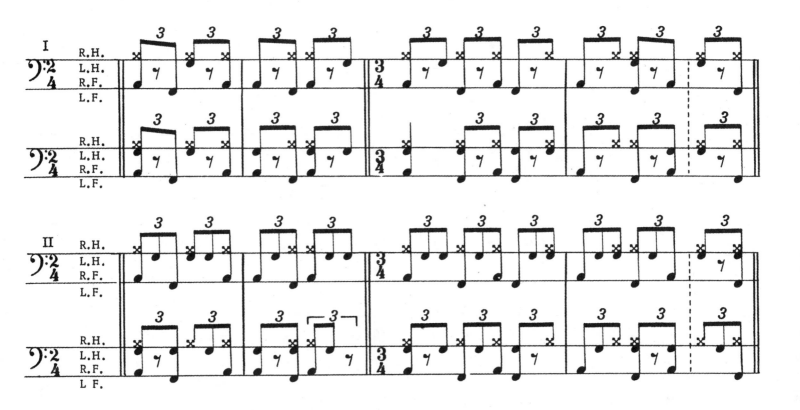

BASIC RHYTHM #18:

BASIC RHYTHM #19:

BASIC RHYTHM #20:

HAB19

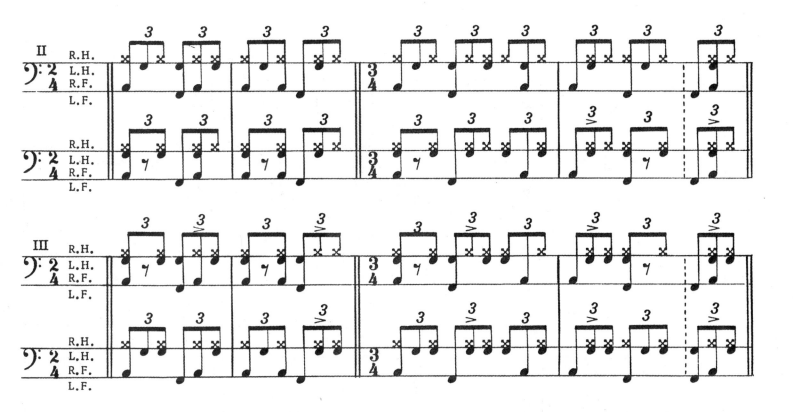

BASIC RHYTHM #21:

HAB19

BASIC RHYTHM #22:

Studies for playing three beat ideas in 4/4 time

On the next page are some examples of a trick used by many modern drummers. It makes use of ideas normally played in 3/4 time put into 4/4 time. A 3-beat idea is played twice. This is preceded or followed by a 2-beat idea to complete a two-measure phrase. Another way to play this is to start with one beat, play two 3-beat ideas and then end with one beat.

Most drummers play a slight accent at the beginning of each 3-beat idea. The right hand plays the cymbal beat like this:

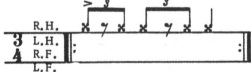

On the next page are some basic rhythms that should be practiced many times until they feel natural. These rhythms are right hand cymbal beats and must be played with a swing.

HAB19

BASIC RHYTHM #1:

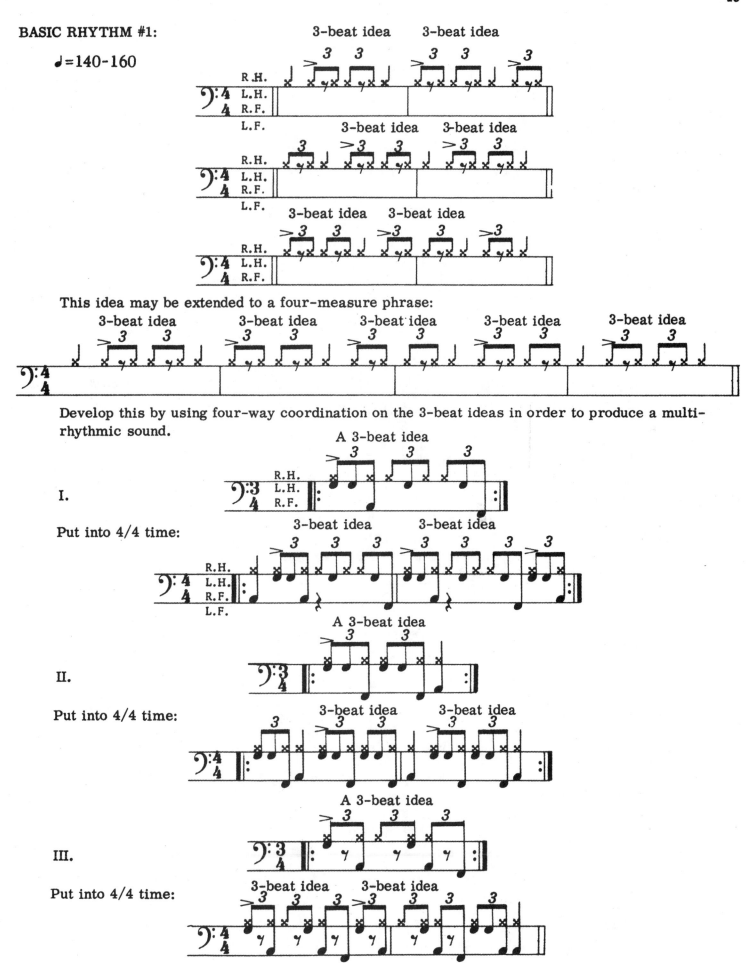

This idea may be extended to a four-measure phrase:

Develop this by using four-way coordination on the 3-beat ideas in order to produce a multi-rhythmic sound.

I.

Put into 4/4 time:

II.

Put into 4/4 time:

III.

Put into 4/4 time:

50

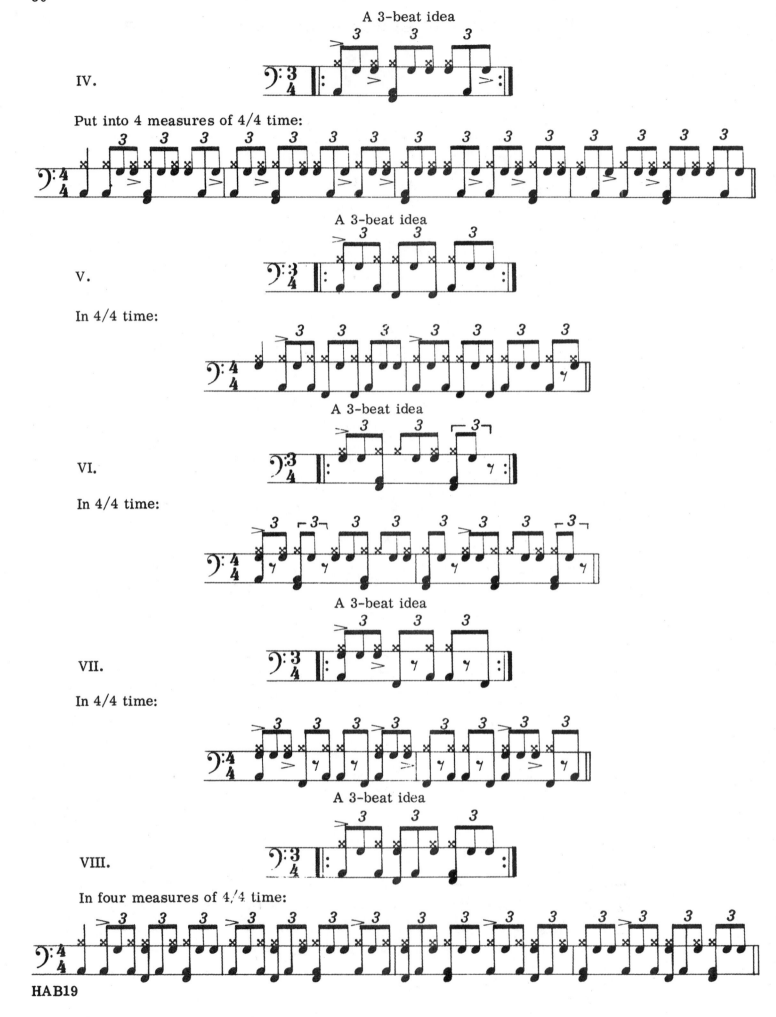

IV.

A 3-beat idea

Put into 4 measures of 4/4 time:

V.

A 3-beat idea

In 4/4 time:

VI.

A 3-beat idea

In 4/4 time:

VII.

A 3-beat idea

In 4/4 time:

VIII.

A 3-beat idea

In four measures of 4/4 time:

Solos written in Complete Independence

The next three pages are solos written in complete independence.

ADVANCED POLYRHYTHMICS

Polyrhythmics means playing two or more independent rhythms at the same time. For the last section of this book, the authors wish to introduce you to a few exercises written in polyrhythmics.

The first page features 8th note triplets played by the hands while the feet play straight 8th notes.

The second page is more complicated and features a separate rhythm for each hand and each foot. The best sound will be obtained if each hand and foot is played on a separate drum or trap.

8th Note Triplets Against 8th Notes (may be considered 12/8 against 4/4)

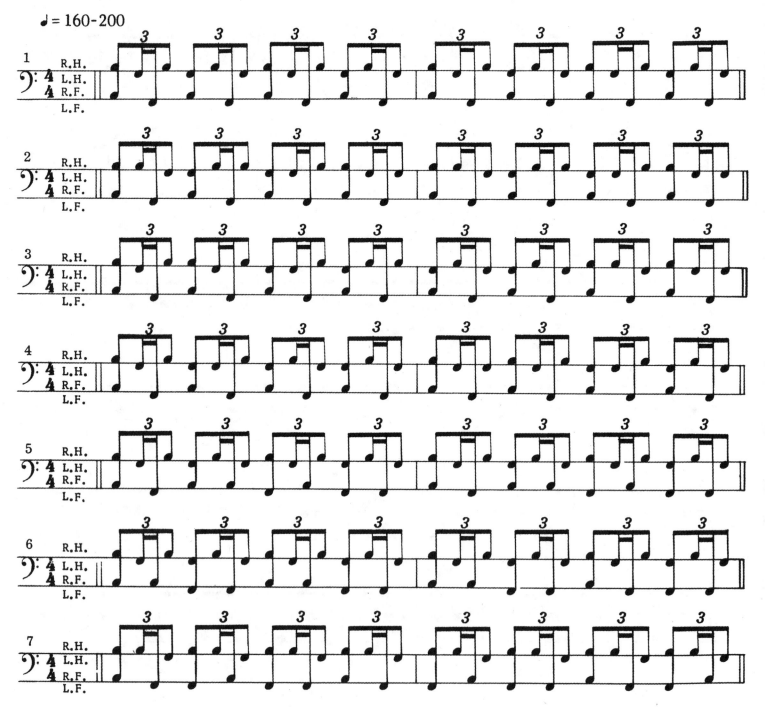

Each exercise written in both 4/4 and 12/8 time: ♩ = ♩.

Ride Cym. (R.H.) in 6 against 9 in L.H. - against 4 in R.F., against 2 in L.F. (on the after beat)

Ride Cym. (R.H.) in 6 - Left hand fill; 4 in R.F., 2 in L.F. (on the after beat)

BOOK II WILL CONTINUE FROM THIS PAGE

PERCUSSION SERIES

DON LAMOND
Written in collaboration with
HENRY ADLER

A series of exercises designed to
enable the Modern Drummer to ac-
quire greater facility on the Drum Set

Every exercise SWINGS!

**by ROY BURNES
and LEWIS MALIN**
Edited by **HENRY ADLER**
**PRACTICAL METHOD OF
DEVELOPING FINGER CONTROL**
A method book that explains step by
step the practical approach to attain
FINGER CONTROL

**by SONNY IGOE
and HENRY ADLER
developing
DRUM BREAKS and FILL-INS**

A series of exercises that enables the
Drummer to play Drum Breaks and
Fill-ins utilizing the entire Drum Set.

**by CHARLES PERRY
Designed for the BEGINNER**

"Two books that really teach the
student to 'get around' on the drums."

VOL. 1 (Elementary)

VOL. 2 (Intermediate)

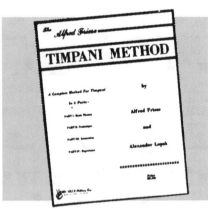

**by ALFRED FRIESE and
ALEXANDER LEPAK**

A complete method for TIMPANI in
4 parts:
BASIC THEORY, TECHNIQUE, IN-
TONATION and REPERTOIRE . . .
written and assembled to fill an
urgent need by America's leading
authorities.

**HUMBERTO MORALES
and HENRY ADLER**

. . . contains a series of exercises
especially written for Latin-American
instruments, together with numerous
illustrations showing the correct
method of playing these instruments.
The text is written in both Spanish
and English.